Audio Access Included – *Recorded Accompaniments Online*

AMERICAN ART SONGS
FOR THE PROGRESSING
MEZZO-SOPRANO

ISBN 978-1-4950-8854-4

To access companion recorded piano accompaniments online, visit:
www.halleonard.com/mylibrary

Enter Code
7715-3676-9506-5431

G. SCHIRMER, Inc.

DISTRIBUTED BY
HAL•LEONARD®
7777 W. BLUEMOUND RD. P.O. BOX 13819 MILWAUKEE, WI 53213

www.musicsalesclassical.com
www.halleonard.com

Pianists on the recordings: [1]Catherine Bringerud, [2]Brendan Fox, [3]Richard Walters, [4]Laura Ward

THE CHILDREN
from *The Children*

Leonard Feeney

Theodore Chanler

Words used by exclusive permission.

We are the chil - dren.

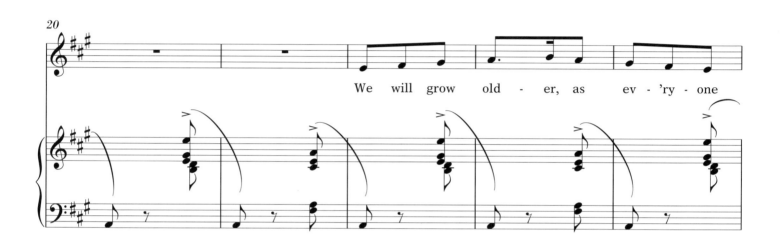

We will grow old - er, as ev - 'ry - one

knows, _____ And when we grow old - er, what

do you sup - pose _____ Will be - come of the

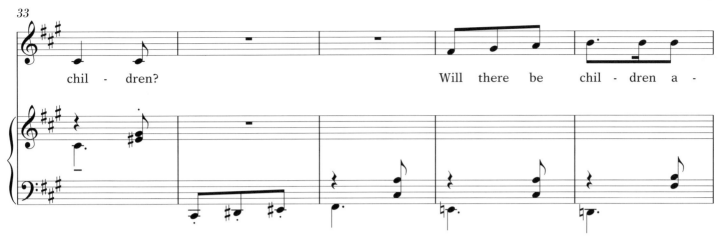

chil - dren? Will there be chil - dren a -

gain, When we who are chil - dren are wo - men and

men? Yes!

Sure - ly the world will love

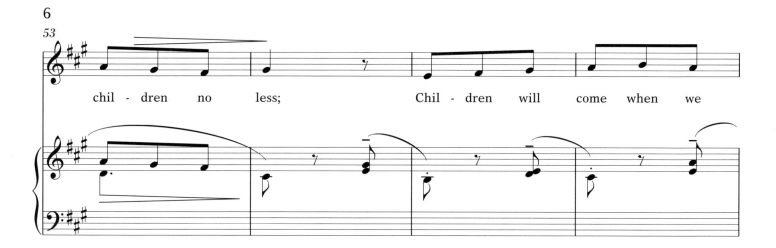

chil - dren no less; Chil - dren will come when we

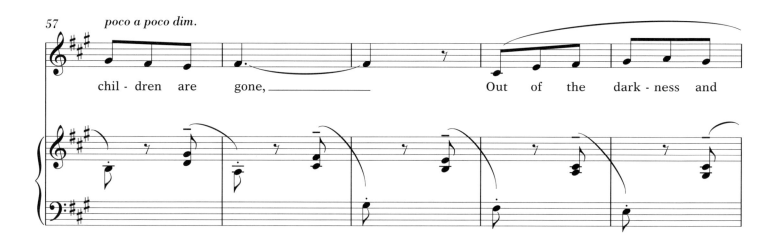

poco a poco dim.

chil - dren are gone, _____ Out of the dark - ness and

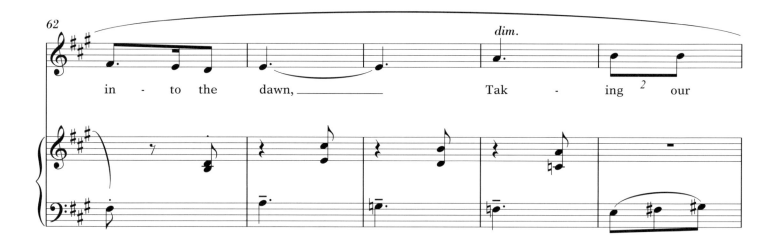

dim.

in - to the dawn, _____ Tak - ing our

p

plac - es, Bear - ing our bright - ness and

leggero

light - ness of limbs, _____ And our laugh - ter and love in their

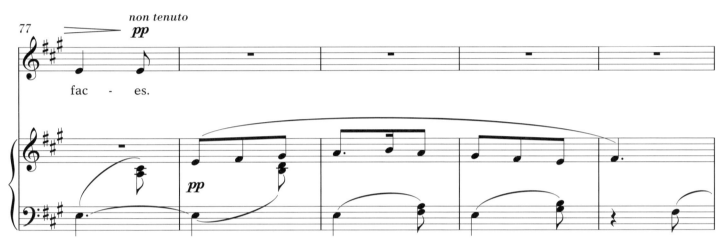

fac - es.

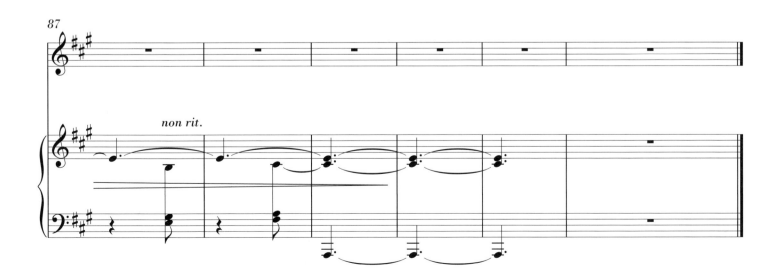

IT'S ALL I HAVE TO BRING

Emily Dickinson*

Ernst Bacon

*Words printed by special permission.

wide. _____ Be sure you count, _____ should I for -

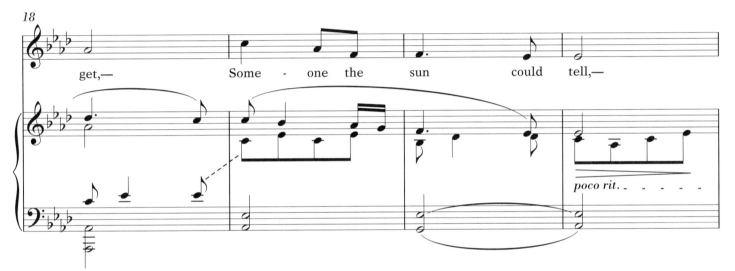

get,— Some - one the sun could tell,—

This, and my heart, and all _____ the bees _____

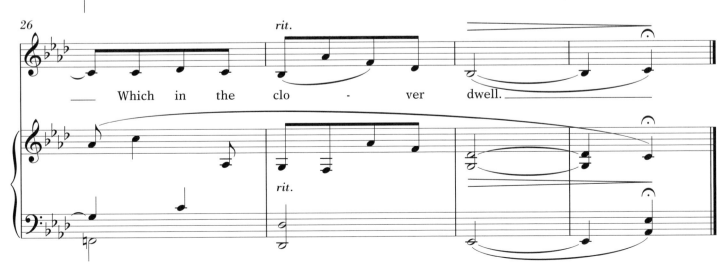

_____ Which in the clo - ver dwell. _____

LONGING
from *Two Poems of the Wind*

Fiona Macleod (William Sharp)

Samuel Barber

Allegro con grazioso

O __ would I were __ the cool __ wind __ that's blow - ing from __ the

sea, ___ Each lone - liest val - ley I would search till I should come to __

thee.＿＿＿＿ In the dew on the grass is your name, dear, i' the

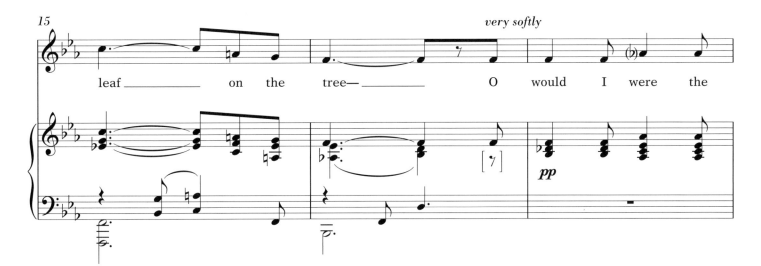

very softly

leaf ＿＿＿ on the tree—＿＿＿ O would I were the

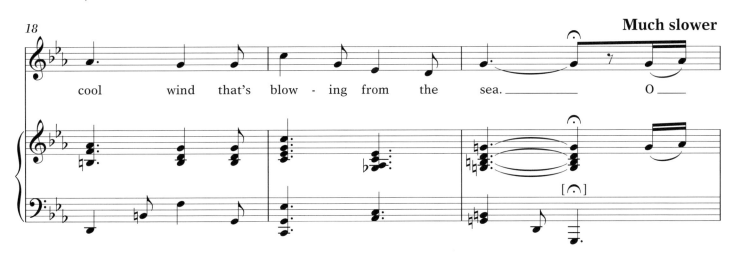

Much slower

cool wind that's blow - ing from the sea.＿＿＿ O ＿＿

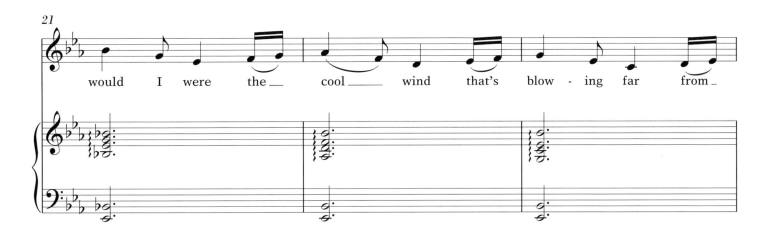

would I were the ＿ cool ＿ wind that's blow - ing far from ＿

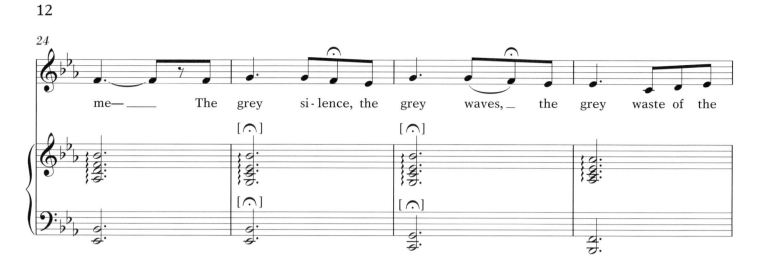

me— The grey si-lence, the grey waves,— the grey waste of the

Tempo I

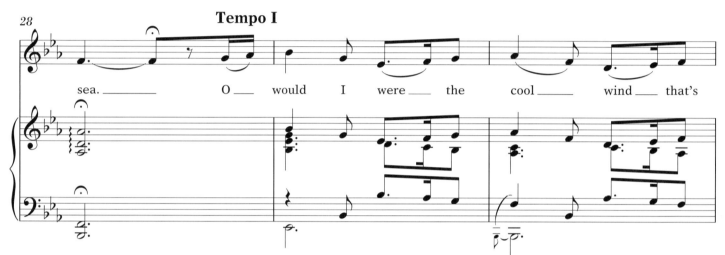

sea._____ O— would I were— the cool— wind— that's

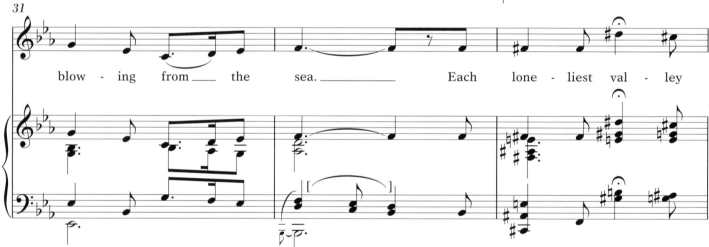

blow-ing from— the sea._____ Each lone-liest val-ley

softly   *rit.*   *opt.**

I would search till I— should come to thee.

rit.

*The optional note appears in Barber's manuscript.

MOTHER, I CANNOT MIND MY WHEEL

Walter Savage Landor

Samuel Barber

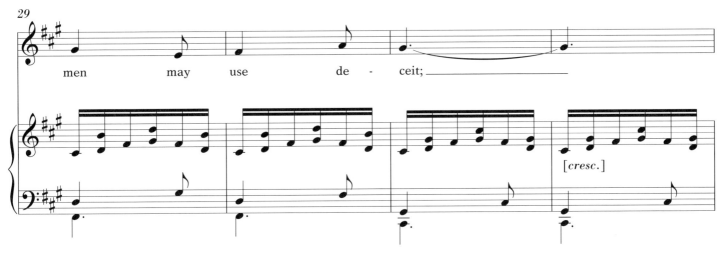

men may use de - ceit; _____

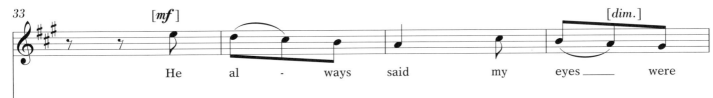

He al - ways said my eyes ____ were

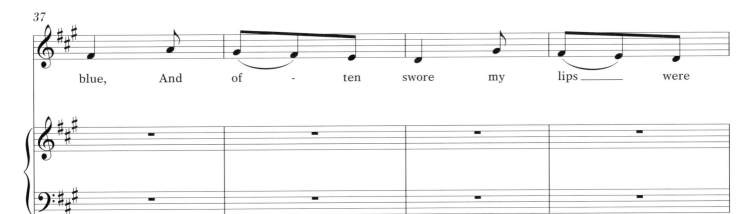

blue, And of - ten swore my lips ____ were

sweet. _____

To Daisy
THE DAISIES
from *Three Songs*

James Stephens

Samuel Barber
Op. 2, No. 1

Poem from *Collected Poems of James Stephens*. Printed by permission of The Macmillan Company, publishers.

wan-dered hap- p'ly,* to and fro; I kissed my dear on ei - ther cheek, In the

bud of the morn - ing— O. A lark sang up from the

breez - y land, A lark sang down from a cloud a - far, As she and

I went hand in hand In the field where the dais - ies are.

The Windmill,
Rogers Park
July 20, 1927

*In Stephens' poem the word is "happily," which Barber chose to set on two notes rather than three.

SOMETIMES I FEEL LIKE A MOTHERLESS CHILD

African-American Spiritual
Arranged by Harry T. Burleigh

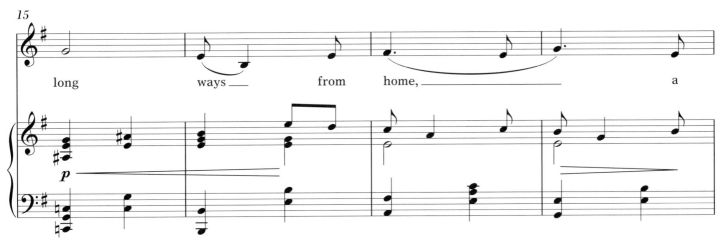

long ways ___ from home, ___ a

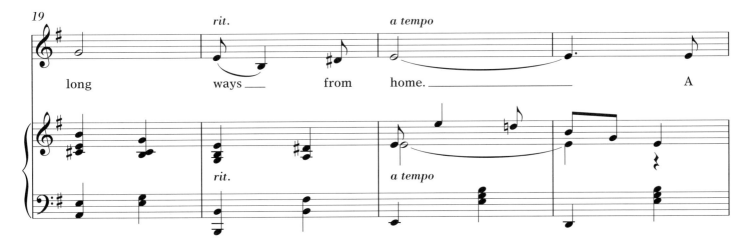

long ways ___ from home. ___ A

long ways ___ from home, ___ a

long ways ___ from home. ___

Some-times I

feel like I'm al - most gone, _____ Some-times I

feel like I'm al - most gone, _____ Some-times I

feel like I'm al - most gone, _____ A long

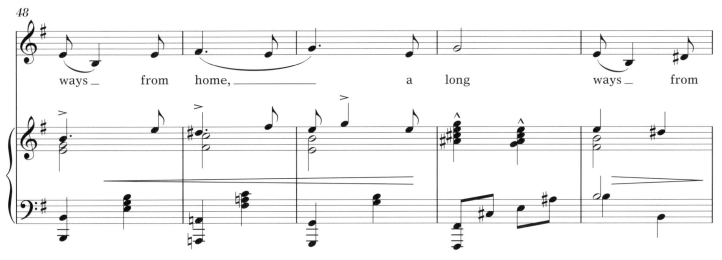

ways __ from home, _____ a long ways __ from

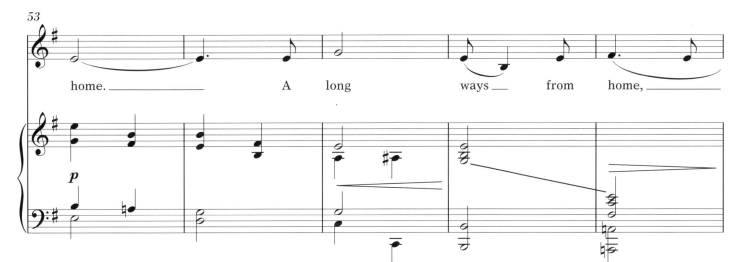

home. _____ A long ways __ from home, _____

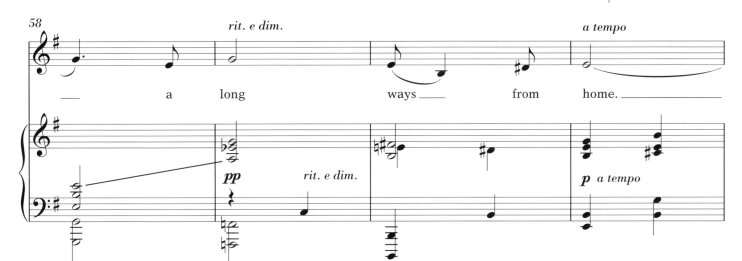

rit. e dim. *a tempo*

a long ways __ from home. _____

To Lawrence Tibbett

LOVELIEST OF TREES

A. E. Housman*

John Duke

* Poem from "A Shropshire Lad." Printed by permission of Grant Richards, London, publisher.

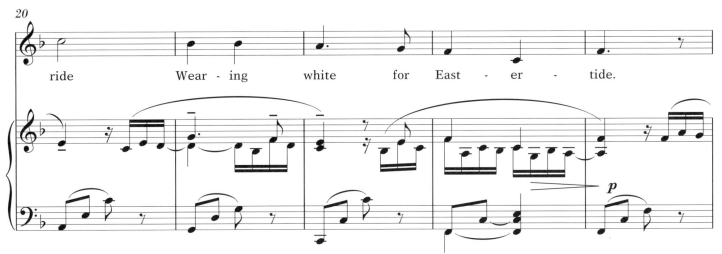

ride   Wear - ing   white   for   East - er - tide.

Now,   of   my   three - score   years   and   ten.

Twen - ty   will   not   come   a - gain,   And

take from sev-en-ty springs a score, It on - ly

leaves me fif - ty more.

And since to look at things in bloom

Fif - ty springs are lit - tle room,

A - bout the wood - lands I will go To

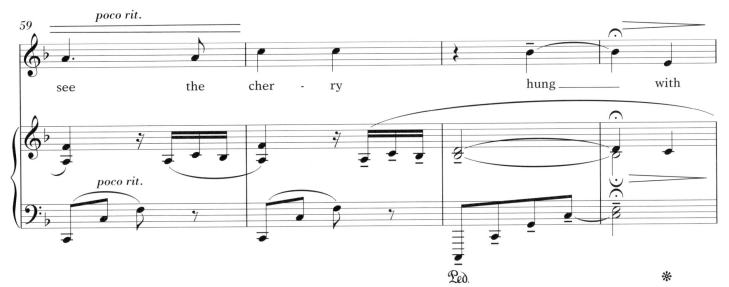

see the cher - ry hung_____ with

snow._____

for Olive Endres

THE SHEPHERD

William Blake

Lee Hoiby

all _ the day _____ And his tongue shall be

filled _____ with praise. _____

For he hears _____ the lamb's in - no - cent call. ____

And _ he hears _____ the ewe's

ten - der _____ re - ply.   He is

watch - ful   when they are in peace,   For they   know   when their

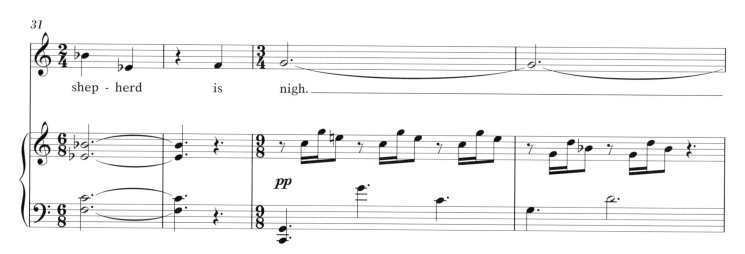

shep - herd   is   nigh. _____

WHERE THE MUSIC COMES FROM

Words and Music by
Lee Hoiby

how. I want to sing to the ear-ly morn - ing, See the

sun - light melt the snow; And oh,_____ I want to

grow._____

I want to

wake   to the liv-ing spir - it   Here in - side   me   where it lies.   I want to

lis - ten till I can hear   it,   Let it guide me, and re - al - ize   That   I can

go   with the flow un - end - ing,   That is blend - ing,   that is

real;   And   oh, _____   I   want   to

de - vas,* to the deer, And to be one with the riv - er flow - ing, Breez - es

blow - ing, sky a - bove;

And oh, I want to love.

*pronounced *day – vas* (nature spirits)

THE LASS FROM THE LOW COUNTREE

Text adapted and Music by
John Jacob Niles

Oh, he was a lord of high de-gree, And she was a lass from the Low Coun-tree, But she loved his lord-ship so ten-der-ly! Oh, sor-row, sing sor-row! Now she

sor - row, sing sor - row! Now she sleeps in the val - ley where the

wild - flow - ers nod, And no one knows she loved him but her -

self and God. _____ If you be a lass from the

Low Coun - tree, Don't love of no lord of _____

8ba _

high de - gree; They hain't got a heart for sym - pa - thy. Oh,

sor - row, sing sor - row! Now she sleeps in the val - ley where the

wild - flow - ers nod. And no one knows she loved him but her -

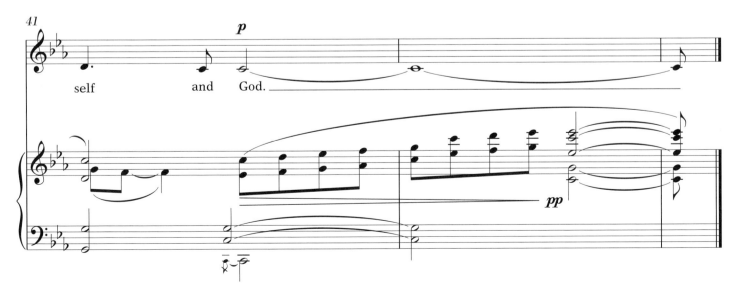

self and God.

to Miriam Witkin

THE GREEN DOG

Words and Music by
Herbert Kingsley

Shoes of leaf - green,

Hose of tea - green, Coat of ap - ple-green, Gloves of bot - tle - green,

In fact, I nev - er would be seen except in

green If my dog were green.

But, a - las! no mat - ter what you've heard, The facts are con - sis - tent - ly ab -

surd, _____ For my dog is - n't green, _____

And, what sets the mat - ter e - ven more a - gog—

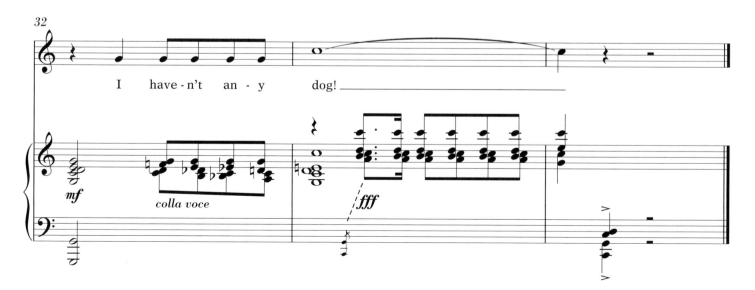

I have - n't an - y dog! _____

to Helen-Claire Moyle

AMERICAN LULLABY

Gladys Rich

week-ly bridge par - ty To get her wee ba - by the prize.

Nurs - ie will turn_ the ra - di - o on,_

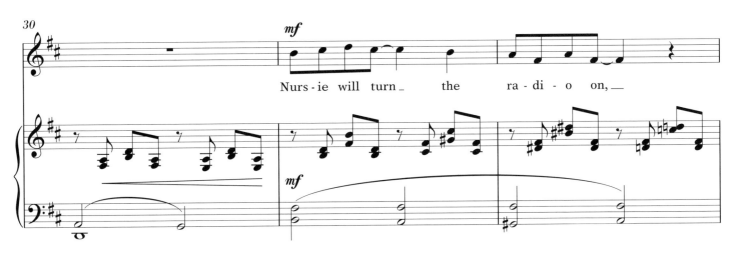

So you can hear_ a sleep-y-time song,_ Sung by a la - dy whose

poor heart must long_ For a ba - by like you!_____

ORPHEUS WITH HIS LUTE

William Shakespeare

William Schuman

show'rs There had made a last-ing spring._____ Ev -'ry thing that heard him

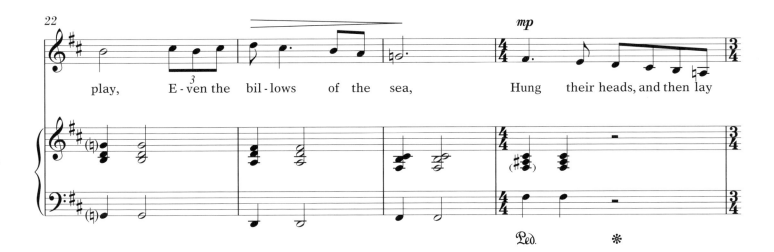

play, E - ven the bil - lows of the sea, Hung their heads, and then lay

by._____ In sweet mu - sic is such art, Kill - ing care and grief of

heart, Fall a - sleep, or hear - ing, die._____

THIS LITTLE ROSE

Emily Dickinson*

William Roy

slightly accelerated

mp

On-ly a bee will miss it, On-ly a but - ter - fly,

p

p

Hast-en ing from far jour - ney On its breast to lie.

slightly accelerated

mp cresc.